MICHAEL JORDAN

by Devra Newberger,
revised and updated
by James Preller

P9-CQD-406

SCHOLASTIC, INC.

New York • Toronto • London • Auckland • Sydney

Photo Credits
Cover: Allsport USA. **Inside front cover:** (top) DUOMO/
Mitchell Layton; (bottom) DUOMO/Adam J. Stoltman.
Inside back cover: (top) DUOMO/William R. Saliaz; (bottom) DUOMO/Ben Van Hook. **iv:** DUOMO/Paul J. Sutton.
6: AP Wide World Photos/Susan Ragan. **11:** AP/Wide
World Photos. **14:** DUOMO/Dan Helms. **20:** DUOMO/
Mitchell Layton. **26:** DUOMO/Ben Van Hook. **30:** AP
Wide World Photos/Michael Conroy. **35:** AP Wide World
Photos/Ruth Fremson. **39, 42:** AP Wide World Photos/
Fred Jewell.

SPORTS SHOTS were conceived by Alan and Marc Boyco.

ISBN 0-590-62327-3

12 11 10 9 8 7 6 5 4 3 2 1   5 6 7 8 9/9 0/0
                                              21
Printed in U.S.A.
First Scholastic printing, October 1995

CONTENTS

CHAPTER ONE
GROWING UP
— 1 —

CHAPTER TWO
HIGH SCHOOL
— 7 —

CHAPTER THREE
COLLEGE DAYS
— 15 —

CHAPTER FOUR
THE PROS
— 21 —

CAREER HIGHLIGHTS
— 43 —

Magic Johnson said it best: "There's Michael, and then there's everybody else."

CHAPTER ONE

GROWING UP

Some people joke that basketball star Michael Jordan was born with wings. It's no joke that this awesome guard for the Chicago Bulls appears to take flight each time he attempts to slam-dunk a basketball. But wings have nothing to do with it. This super player worked long and hard to master the game of basketball.

Determination, not wings, "Air" Jordan explains, is how a normal kid from North Carolina learned to "fly."

Michael Jeffrey Jordan was born in

Brooklyn, New York, on February 17, 1963. He was still an infant when his parents packed up their five kids and moved to Wilmington, North Carolina. It was there that Michael grew up.

The Jordan household was filled with love and warmth. Michael's parents believed in supporting and encouraging their children and taught them the importance of striving to achieve their dreams.

"The way it is in our family," Michael's father once explained, "is that we try to make something happen rather than waiting around for it to happen. We believe the surest way is to work toward making it the way you want it."

"I was lucky," Michael says about his parents. "They gave me guidance and taught me to work hard."

Michael will tell you that his mom and dad instilled their best qualities into their son. He also picked up a few other things from his parents, like his habit of sticking out his tongue when playing basketball! His dad had this same habit while working in the backyard or fixing the family car. Since father and son spent so much time together, Michael picked up the same habit. Today he is famous for the way he dribbles downcourt with his tongue wagging.

"I've been doing it for so long now that it's a habit I just can't stop," he remarks. Michael worries about kids imitating this habit. "If kids try to do it, and they bite their tongues," he says, "that's something I don't want to be the cause of."

Many people say that Michael has become a role model for kids. He agrees, and takes this role very seriously. He is pleased that kids try to be like him. For that reason, he is careful in the things that he says and does. He doesn't smoke. He doesn't drink. And he'd never do drugs. "I know how positive I want my lifestyle to be," Michael says seriously, "and that's the way I live it."

Surprisingly, Michael was a shy and insecure child. He says he felt especially uncomfortable around girls; that they thought he was "gooney."

"A lot of guys picked on me," recalls Michael, "and they would do it in front of the girls. They would joke about my hair-cut and the way that I played with my tongue out; all different things. The girls would laugh. I couldn't get a date with anybody!"

He was more comfortable at home, playing with his brothers and sisters. Michael and his older brothers, James Jr. and Larry, shared a love for sports — all sports. Michael and Larry played basketball together in a local league when Michael was seven or eight years old. Surprisingly enough, Larry was the basketball star of the family and went on to be a star player at Laney High School in Wilmington. Michael joined Little League instead!

Michael remembers that he was a pretty good pitcher. His best childhood sports memory is the one-hitter he pitched when he was 12 years old. He was voted Most Valuable Player after the game. He even won a scholarship to the Mickey Owen baseball camp.

By junior high school, Michael was an all-around athlete. He pitched and played outfield on the baseball team, quarterbacked the football team, and was a guard on the school basketball team.

Michael Jordan was on his way.

Michael starred on the 1984 United States Olympic basketball team, then returned for more gold in 1992 with the "Dream Team."

CHAPTER TWO
HIGH SCHOOL

Meanwhile, Larry was still the star player on the high school varsity basketball team. Michael was proud of his older brother, but also envied him. While Michael was a good basketball player, he felt he needed to grow taller to play for the high school varsity team. But that didn't seem likely. No one in the Jordan family was more than six feet tall!

Michael worked hard on his basketball skills. To compensate for his lack of height, he strove to improve his vertical leap.

Michael's dad saw how serious Michael had become about basketball and built a court in their backyard. Michael spent so much time practicing on his new court, he wore away the grass!

"We played neighborhood games for at least two hours every day, and on Saturdays we were out there all day," he says. He liked to play with guys who were bigger and better than he. Michael thinks that playing with the big boys helped make him a better player.

All that practice did make a difference. Yet no matter how hard he tried, Michael still couldn't beat Larry in a game of one-on-one. It practically drove him crazy! But his drive and determination made him try even harder. "Michael got his competitive nature from his mother," said his dad.

On the other hand, Michael credits those one-on-one games with Larry as the driving force behind his will to improve. "Larry always used to beat me on the backyard court," Michael says. "His vertical jump is higher than mine. He's got the dunks and some three-six-ties and most of the same stuff I have. And he's only five-seven! He's my inspiration."

When Michael entered his sophomore year at Laney High, he still wasn't good enough to make the varsity team. He played junior varsity instead, but wasn't happy about it.

Meanwhile, Michael made the varsity *football* team! He also made the track team, where he excelled in — what else? — the high jump!

But Michael still worked long and hard to improve his basketball game. He even cut a few classes in order to practice, and as a result, was suspended from school three times!

Luckily, his dad stepped in to set Michael straight. James Sr. firmly suggested that Michael reevaluate his goals. When Michael explained that he had hopes of going to college to play basketball, his father told him that if he continued to do poorly in school, no college would want him.

"I knew he was right and I tried to change," Michael says. "I concentrated more on my schoolwork. I had a goal and I knew I had to work to reach it."

Then a miracle happened. That summer, before he was to enter his junior year, he grew four inches! Michael was 6'3" tall on the first day of school. "It was almost as if Michael just willed himself taller," his father said.

Some habits are hard to break. A youthful Michael Jordan lets it all hang out on the basketball court.

When basketball season began that year, Michael finally made the varsity team. Michael's practice routine was an exhausting one. From five until seven o'clock in the evening, he joined the junior varsity team's practice — and then stayed on to practice with the varsity team until nine. Saturdays and Sundays he played all day long.

His persistence paid off. During the holiday tournament that winter, Michael had his first moment in the spotlight. Laney was playing arch-rival New Hanover High School — and Michael scored his team's final 15 points, sinking a jump shot at the buzzer to win the game!

Michael continued his strenuous regimen of basketball practice and schoolwork throughout his senior year. Soon Michael had a new goal — to get a college basketball scholarship. And from the way he was playing during his last season at Laney, there was no doubt that many colleges would try to recruit him.

When the offers came pouring in, Michael found himself faced with a big decision. Which school should he go to?

He had always been a big fan of North Carolina State University because his basketball hero, David Thompson, played there. But his mom was a big fan of the University of North Carolina (UNC), which had one of the best basketball programs in the nation.

Michael didn't make up his mind until he visited the UNC campus at Chapel Hill. Needless to say, he made his mom very happy when he accepted a UNC scholarship for the following fall.

"After my first game as a player on the Tar Heels," said Michael, "I realized I was as good as anybody else."

CHAPTER THREE

COLLEGE DAYS

Fall 1981 arrived, and Michael started school as an official member of the University of North Carolina basketball team — the Tar Heels. At first, he was scared that he wouldn't be good enough. UNC had recruited some of the best high school basketball talent in the country.

But when the season began, Michael found himself named to the Tar Heels starting lineup. It was quite an accomplishment. Usually freshmen are stationed on the bench to watch and learn from their more experienced, older teammates. But there would be no bench sitting for Michael Jordan!

College life treated Michael well. He did a terrific job on the basketball court *and* in the classroom. Maintaining a B average, Michael declared a major in geography. Michael enjoyed the social aspect of college life, as well. He shared an apartment with teammate Buzz Peterson, and the two became best friends. They spent their free time together, playing cards or Monopoly, dating, or hitting the golf course — another of Michael's passions.

If you've ever heard the phrase "that championship season," you have an idea of exactly what kind of year Michael had. In fact, one of the most exciting moments in college basketball history happened during Michael's freshman year — with Michael right in the thick of the action!

The night was March 29, 1982, and the Tar Heels were playing the Georgetown Hoyas to decide the NCAA national champion. A crowd of 61,612 fans packed into the Superdome in New Orleans to witness the game. Millions more watched on television.

The Tar Heels were the number-one team in the country. The Hoyas, who were known for their tough, physical style of play, were number six. They also had seven-foot star center Patrick Ewing, nicknamed the "Hoya Destroyer." Today Ewing plays for the New York Knicks.

From the start of the game, there was electricity in the air. Everyone was charged up; at times the noise reached deafening decibels. The game itself was fast and furious. Both teams played nose-to-nose, trading baskets to the crowd's delight.

With less than a minute left, UNC had the ball, trailing 62-61. They needed a basket to win. They passed the ball around, hoping to get it to their best player, James Worthy (who would later star for the Los Angeles Lakers alongside Magic Johnson and Kareem Abdul-Jabbar). But Worthy was so heavily covered that he couldn't shoot. Worthy desperately looked around and saw Jordan open near the baseline. He passed him the ball and — with only 16 seconds left — Michael swished a 17-foot jump shot to give UNC the national title, 63-62!

That shot changed Michael's life. From that moment on, he was famous. He won All-America honors and was named the Atlantic Coast Conference Rookie of the Year. And those were just the first of many awards to come.

Michael had great seasons in both his sophomore and junior years. But soon he was faced with a big decision. He knew that staying at UNC and playing college basketball would only slow his development as a player, so he decided to leave school after his junior year and join the National Basketball Association (NBA).

The summer before joining the NBA, Michael led the United States basketball team to a gold medal at the Summer Olympics in Los Angeles, California. Michael had achieved everything he could as an amateur player. And now, as always, Michael set new goals for himself. It was time to test his talents against the best players in the world.

Michael soars in for a monster jam. His fierce competitive nature helps make him great.

CHAPTER FOUR

THE PROS

When the Chicago Bulls drafted Michael Jordan with the third pick in the 1984 NBA draft, they were desperate for a player who could turn the team around. And Michael did just that.

In his rookie year, Michael averaged 28.2 points a game, third best in the NBA. He was named Rookie of the Year and an All-Star.

Although injured most of his second season, Michael was ready to face the Bulls' first-round play-off opponent, the Boston Celtics. In game two, Michael poured in a record-setting 63 points. It was a legendary performance. Still the Bulls lost the game and the series, three games to none. "Forget the record," Michael said. "I'd give all the points back if we could win."

Many more personal records came, but Michael would only be satisfied with a championship. Michael hungered for team — not merely individual — success. The Bulls' inability to win a championship led some to suggest that Michael wasn't a great leader like Larry Bird or Magic Johnson, players who had carried their teams to the top. After more failures in the 1989 and 1990 play-offs, Michael grew even more determined to prove the critics wrong.

Behind Michael's fierce leadership, the Chicago Bulls won it all in 1991, topping the Los Angeles Lakers. Michael played some of the finest basketball of his career. Moments after winning the title, he said, "It means so much. When I first got to Chicago, we started at the bottom. Every year we worked harder and harder till we got to the top."

The Bulls came back in 1992 with a single goal in mind — to repeat that championship season. Featuring a more balanced team than ever before — with clutch performances by fellow starters Horace Grant, Scottie Pippen, BJ Armstrong, and Bill Cartwright — Michael led the Bulls to an incredible 67-15 record. They went on to beat the Portland Trail Blazers, four games to two, in the NBA finals.

Then again, in 1993 — for an amazing third championship in a row! — the Bulls beat Charles Barkley and the Phoenix Suns. In each championship series,

Michael was named Most Valuable Player. The critics were silenced. Michael stood at the top of the mountain, clearly the best player in the NBA — possibly the best of all time.

Off the court, Michael was scoring big, too. Companies clamored to have him endorse their products. His face graced cereal boxes, and fast food and soft drink commercials. When Nike began making Air Jordan sneakers, sales soared just like Mike's high-flying dunks.

Then tragedy struck. In July 1993, Michael's father was murdered during a robbery. Michael retreated to the support and strength of his family. Despite their sorrow, Michael and his family maintained a positive outlook. "Dad is no longer with us," they wrote in a public statement. "The lessons he taught us will remain with us forever and they will give us the strength to move forward with a renewed sense of purpose in our lives."

On October 6, 1993 — just a month before the 1993-1994 season was to begin — Michael shocked the sports world by announcing his retirement at age 30. He told reporters, "I've accomplished everything I set out to do. I just don't have anything left to prove."

Before his retirement, Chicago looked unstoppable. The Bulls had charged through the league three straight years, registering a record of 185-61 in the regular season, 45-13 in the play-offs, during that span. And with a core of Michael Jordan, Scottie Pippen, and Horace Grant, they looked solid for years to come. Without Michael, the team could not hope to reach the same heights.

Meanwhile, Michael rocked the sports

Batter up! Michael shocked the sports world when he hung up his high-tops and put on baseball cleats.

world again when he turned his talents to a new challenge — baseball! Perhaps it was a result of the death of his father, who was an avid baseball fan. Perhaps he was simply following a childhood dream. But Michael Jordan — King of the Blacktop — turned in his high-tops for cleats. His goal? Nothing less than making it to the major leagues. An almost unthinkable ambition — especially for a 31-year-old basketball player who hadn't played organized baseball since high school!

Some critics considered it a bad joke. It seemed ridiculous that the world's greatest hoopster would risk embarrassing himself on the baseball diamond. But Michael was serious.

He struggled from the start. It had been a long time between fastballs. The rust showed. He finished the 1993 baseball season playing for the Scottsdale Scorpions of the Arizona Fall League. In 35 games, he hit .252 with no homers.

He returned to play a full season for the Double A Birmingham Barons in 1994. It was a difficult year. Michael hit only .202 for the season. He played in 127 games, got 88 hits in 436 at bats, with 3 homers, 51 RBIs, 30 stolen bases, 14 strikeouts, and 11 errors. Yet he showed signs of improvement. Some coaches believed that Michael just might pull off this impossible dream.

Of course, the basketball superstar had to adjust to life as a minor league baseball player. It wasn't easy. "My success in basketball was so rapid," he said. "Here, obviously, it's not. I have had to deal with a lot more disappointment."

Baseball itself offered more disappointments. A bitter strike had cut short the 1994 major league season and threatened the beginning of the 1995 season. It made Michael uneasy. On March 2, 1995, he packed his things and left camp. The great baseball experiment was over.

Rumors began circulating daily. "He's coming back," people said. Newspapers ran front-page stories. Michael was seen practicing with his former teammates. Could it be true? Could he be returning to basketball? Now, after being away for almost eighteen months? Michael wasn't saying.

Finally, on March 18, 1995, Michael released the following two-word statement to the press: "I'm back."

Those two little words sent shock waves through the NBA. Michael had ended his flirtation with baseball. He was returning to the game he loved. Said

Michael returned to basketball against the Indiana Pacers. After losing a close game, he said, "I'm back. That's all that matters."

Michael, "I came back for the love of the game. Because I started to miss it more and more. And with the baseball strike, I wasn't comfortable anymore in the baseball setting."

Needless to say, the Chicago Bulls — and their fans — were ecstatic. Will Perdue, backup center for the Bulls, had the best line: "I have only three words to say about it. Thank you, baseball!!"

Michael was set to play his first game back against the Indiana Pacers. The excitement was incredible. Everywhere people went, they talked about his return. Ticket scalpers asked for — and got! — as much as $680 for a $42 ticket. Everyone wanted to see the most famous athlete on the face of the earth play basketball once more.

There was something different about Michael that first game. Yes, he had the old moves, the same wagging tongue, the same intensity. What was it? His uniform. Michael changed his number from the familiar No. 23 to No. 45! He explained, "Twenty-three was the number my father last saw me in, and I wanted to keep it that way for him."

As expected, Michael was not at the top of his game. He missed his first six shots from the field, finishing the day with a mortal 19 points in 43 minutes. Chicago lost 103-96, in overtime. But no one seemed to mind. Only one thing mattered: *He was back.*

In just his fifth game back, Michael found himself in Madison Square Garden, squaring off against the arch-rival New York Knicks.

It was to be a game for the ages — one of the most spectacular individual performances of all time. The crowd sat spellbound as Michael poured in basket after basket. He had 49 points after three quarters. He was a wizard — pump-faking, making spin moves, driving hard to the hoop, soaring high, and nailing three-pointers. As the last seconds of the game ticked away, the score was tied and Michael had the ball. Double-teamed by the shell-shocked Knicks, Michael passed off to Bill Wennington for an easy, game-ending stuff. The Bulls won 113-111. Michael ended up with 55 points, the most ever scored in Madison Square Garden, hitting 21 of 37 field goals, and 10 of 11 free throws.

Said John Starks, the Knick assigned to guard Jordan, "I tried. I tried to throw everything I had at him. It was a matter of time before he played one of those games like you just weren't there."

Suddenly, the also-ran Bulls were on

fire. Brimming with new confidence, they looked to the play-offs with new hope. Steve Kerr, a backup guard for the Bulls, said it this way: "Right now, we have a lot of confidence. We have Superman on our side."

Superman or not, basketball is still a team game, played five against five. Before Michael's return, the Bulls were in fourth place, floundering near .500. They had lost their great power forward, Horace Grant, to the Orlando Magic. The team had many shortcomings: They ranked near the bottom in rebounding; their scoring was inconsistent; they bickered and seemed to lack focus.

Could Michael Jordan alone cure the ills of this team?

Without question, his presence made the Bulls better — much, much better. But Michael cautioned, "I have to learn

Michael towers over 5'3" Muggsy Bogues during the play-offs against the Charlotte Hornets.

who my new teammates are and how to play with them. And they've got to play with me. But it's going to take more than five guys to win a championship. It's going to take a whole team effort."

The Bulls cruised into the play-offs having won 13 and lost only 4 since Michael's return. They took the opening best-of-five series against the Charlotte Hornets, three games to one. Still, the Bulls played only well enough to win. No one mistook this group for the great Bulls teams of old.

The next round would be the true test, for they were set to square off against the up-and-coming Orlando Magic. Led by Shaquille O'Neal, Anfernee Hardaway, and ex-Bull Horace Grant, the Magic were young, strong, and hungry for a title.

The first game was in Orlando. In a

much-talked-about moment, as Michael stood at the foul line, an Orlando fan raised a hand-lettered sign that read: NO. 23 WAS GREAT. NO. 45 IS JUST AVERAGE.

And — for some — it seemed about right. Superman looked human, beatable. In a disastrous game, Michael shot 8-for-22, committing eight turnovers, two in the final 10 seconds. The Bulls lost, 94-91. Michael was the goat.

Many wondered: Had age taken its toll? The old Michael Jordan never seemed to fail. No. 23 was the greatest ever. Could this No. 45 — fumbling in the closing seconds of a tense play-off game — be the same legend? Nick Anderson, who guarded Michael in that game, said, "Number forty-five isn't like number twenty-three. He used to take off like the space shuttle. He would blow right by you. Now he's revving up trying to get ready and not really taking off."

Michael heard the criticism — and it stung him. So he planned a surprise of his own for game two. Michael brought No. 23 out of mothballs and played like his old self. He scored 38 points and controlled the game from the opening tipoff to the closing buzzer. He was inspired, snaring seven rebounds, stealing the ball four times, and blocking four shots in 43 minutes of play. The Bulls evened the series at one game apiece.

Said Michael of the uniform switch, "I'm going to stick with twenty-three until I finish playing basketball. That's me. Twenty-three is me. So why try to be something else, even though I know my father has never seen me in forty-five."

The series battled on. Orlando took game three, but Chicago roared right

After a disappointing play-off elimination, Michael promised to return next year — for another championship ring!

back to win game four. Led by Horace Grant, Orlando dominated the boards and won game five. Trailing three games to two, Michael and the Bulls returned to Chicago to play a must-win sixth game. The Bulls felt confident. They were home. And Superman was on their side.

It was not meant to be.

The Orlando Magic brought high-flying Michael Jordan down to earth, winning 108-102. Obviously weary by the fourth quarter, Michael managed to chip in an ordinary 23 points. It wasn't enough. The load was too heavy. Even for Superman. Basketball still is, after all, a team game. Played five-on-five. The Bulls just didn't have what it took.

Although his Chicago Bulls failed in the play-offs, Michael Jordan got exactly what he wanted. For there he was — diving for loose balls, racing upcourt for a gravity-defying jam, soaring high, flicking his wrist, and letting the ball go. Nothing but net.

Yes, Michael had missed the thrill of the game. And, most certainly, the game missed Michael. Win or lose, it doesn't matter. Not really. Because the greatest to ever play the game is back where he belongs: *On the court.*

His Airness flies to the hoop; all is right in the NBA.

CAREER HIGHLIGHTS

- Was a member of the University of North Carolina's NCAA-championship winning team and the ACC Rookie of the Year: 1982.

- *Sporting News* College Player of the Year, 1983-1984.

- NBA Rookie of the Year: 1984-1985.

- Scored 3,041 points in 1986-1987, the highest season total for a guard in NBA history.

- NBA Most Valuable Player: 1988, 1991, and 1992.

- Most Valuable Player in the NBA championship series: 1991, 1992, and 1993. (No other player has even won the award two times in a row.)

- Member gold-medal-winning Olympic Dream Team: 1992.

- Seven-time consecutive NBA Scoring Leader (tied with Wilt Chamberlain for the record): 1987-1993.

- Reached 20,000-point level (1993) faster than any player except Wilt Chamberlain.

- Scored personal high 69 points versus Cleveland: March 28, 1990.

- Named All-Defense first team six straight years: 1988-1993.

- Highest scoring average, NBA Finals, 41.0 against Phoenix: 1993.